Before They Were President

BEFORE GEORGE WASHINGTON WAS PRESIDENT

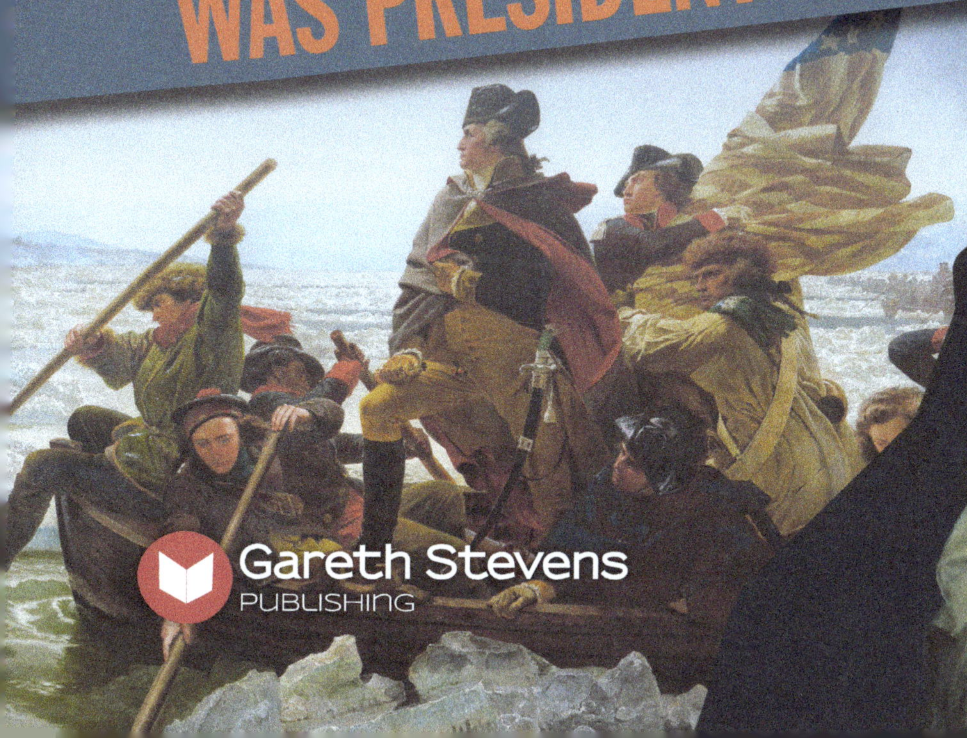

Gareth Stevens PUBLISHING

By Janey Levy

Please visit our website, www.garethstevens.com. For a free color catalog of all our high-quality books, call toll free 1-800-542-2595 or fax 1-877-542-2596.

Cataloging-in-Publication Data
Names: Levy, Janey.
Title: Before George Washington was president / Janey Levy.
Description: New York : Gareth Stevens Publishing, 2019. | Series: Before they were president | Includes glossary and index.
Identifiers: ISBN 9781538232545 (pbk.) | ISBN 9781538229125 (library bound) | ISBN 9781538232552 (6pack)
Subjects: LCSH: Washington, George, 1732-1799–Juvenile literature. | Washington, George, 1732-1799–Childhood and youth–Juvenile literature. | Presidents–United States–Biography–Juvenile literature.
Classification: LCC E312.2 L48 2019 | DDC 973.4'1092 B–dc23

First Edition

Published in 2019 by
Gareth Stevens Publishing
111 East 14th Street, Suite 349
New York, NY 10003

Designer: Laura Bowen
Editor: Therese Shea

Photo credits: Cover, p. 1 (Washington portrait) John Parrot/Stocktrek Images/Getty Images; cover, p. 1 (background) The Metropolitan Museum of Art/Aavindraa/Wikimedia Commons; cover, pp. 1–21 (frame) Samran wonglakorn/Shutterstock.com; p. 5 (main) The Athenaeum/Alonso de Mendoza/Wikimedia Commons; p. 5 (inset) Robert Edge Pine/BaomoVW/Wikimedia Commons; p. 7 (main) Lawrence Thornton/Archive Photos/Getty Images; p. 7 (inset) John C. McRae/Materialscientist/Wikimedia Commons; p. 9 (map) Ingo Menhard/Shutterstock.com; p. 9 (young Washington) National Park Service, U.S. Dept. of the Interior/Realtube/Wikimedia Commons; p. 11 Charles Willson Peale/Scewing/Wikimedia Commons; p. 13 (family) Everett Historical/Shutterstock.com; p. 13 (inset) J. Cheney & J. G. Kellogg/Centpacrr/Wikimedia Commons; p. 15 Photo Josse/Leemage/Corbis Historical/Getty Images; p. 17 John Trumball/Zeete/Wikimedia Commons; p. 19 bodhichita/Shutterstock.com; p. 21 (top) Fæ/Wikimedia Commons; p. 21 (bottom) Hugo Brizard/Shutterstock.com.

Printed in the United States of America

CPSIA compliance information: Batch #CW19GS: For further information contact Gareth Stevens, New York, New York at 1-800-542-2595.

CONTENTS

Words in the glossary appear in **bold** type the first time they are used in the text.

THE WASHINGTON YOU DON'T KNOW

Everyone knows George Washington was the first president of the United States. But many people don't know much about his life before he was president.

Washington was born in the British colony of Virginia on February 22, 1732. This was before the country of the United States even existed. As a young man seeking adventure, he wanted to join the navy. However, his mother wouldn't let him. He later became a **surveyor**, military officer, and farmer. Are you curious to learn more? Keep reading!

Presidential Preview

Young George Washington copied the 110 rules in a book called *The Rules of* ***Civility*** *and* ***Decent*** *Behaviour in Company and Conversation*, which explained how to be a good person. It's believed this had a big effect on his character.

THIS IS THE KIND OF PICTURE OF GEORGE WASHINGTON MOST PEOPLE KNOW BEST. IT WAS PAINTED WHILE HE WAS PRESIDENT.

GEORGE'S MOTHER, MARY BALL WASHINGTON

YOUNG WASHINGTON

We don't know much about George Washington's youth. Some of what people think they know is wrong. The story about young George chopping down a cherry tree isn't true. It was made up by someone who wrote about his life later.

We do know George grew up on Ferry Farm near Fredericksburg, Virginia. Because George's father died when he was 11, George didn't get as much education as his older brothers. But he learned how to care for the farm and to become a surveyor.

Presidential Preview

After his father's death, Washington **inherited** Ferry Farm as well as 10 slaves.

GEORGE'S FATHER, AUGUSTINE WASHINGTON

THIS BUILDING ON FERRY FARM WAS SAID TO BE WASHINGTON'S SURVEYING OFFICE, BUT OTHERS DON'T THINK IT EXISTED BACK THEN.

WASHINGTON'S FIRST JOB

Are you good at math? Young George Washington was, and it helped him learn surveying, which became his first job. In 1748, he was only 16 years old when he spent a month helping survey land in the Shenandoah (sheh-nuhn-DOH-uh) Valley.

In 1749, 17-year-old Washington became the official surveyor of Culpeper County. He held this position for more than 2 years. But his life soon changed. Washington's brother Lawrence died in 1752, and he left his large Mount Vernon **estate** to Washington.

Presidential Preview

Washington kept a diary of his surveying trip to the Shenandoah Valley. He wrote about sleeping under a blanket covered with bugs, having no dishes to eat from, and meeting a Native American war party.

Washington's Virginia

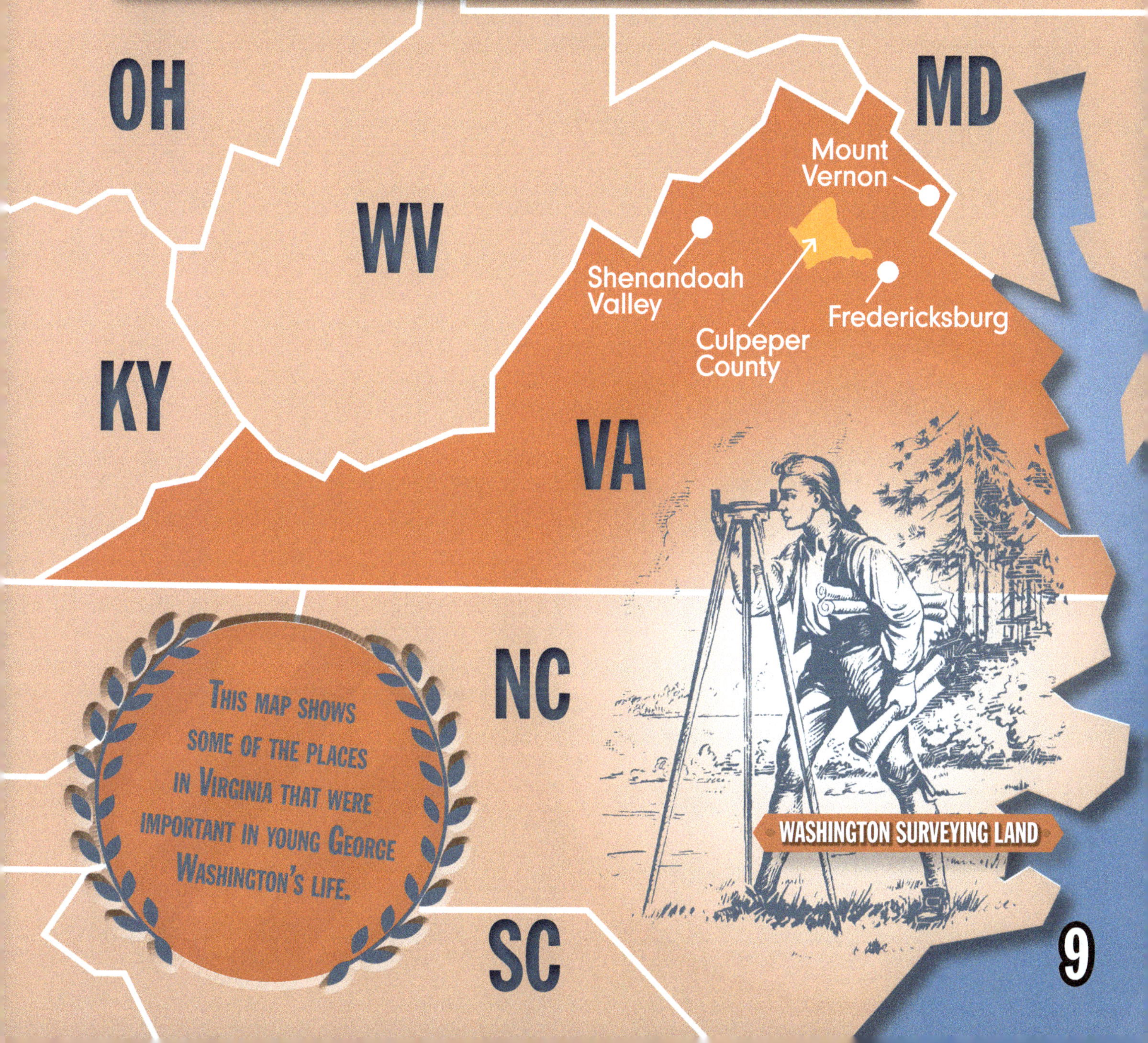

This map shows some of the places in Virginia that were important in young George Washington's life.

WASHINGTON SURVEYING LAND

WAR BRINGS CHANGE

Soon after Washington inherited Mount Vernon, war spread over the colonies. England and France both claimed the land that's now western Pennsylvania because it offered excellent trade opportunities. What's now known as the French and Indian War broke out between the two countries in 1754.

Washington was only 22 and had no military experience. However, he became an important leader for the colony of Virginia during the war. After peace returned to Virginia in 1758, Washington left the military and returned to Mount Vernon.

Presidential Preview

Washington sometimes made poor choices as a young leader and didn't always win his battles. However, he showed great courage during fighting.

HERE'S WASHINGTON IN THE UNIFORM HE WORE WHILE FIGHTING AGAINST THE FRENCH.

WASHINGTON GETS MARRIED

George Washington wanted a family to complete his life at Mount Vernon. On January 6, 1759, he married Martha Dandridge Custis. It was Washington's first marriage and Martha's second. She was a wealthy young **widow** with a large estate and two small children.

Martha's estate made Washington richer. But her young children were more important to him. He grew to love Martha's son Jacky and her daughter Patsy as his own. He gave them lots of attention and worried when they had problems.

Presidential Preview

Patsy died a few years before the **American Revolution**, and Jacky died near the end of the war. Jacky left behind four children, and Washington and Martha adopted two of them.

GEORGE AND MARTHA, WITH GRANDCHILDREN

MARTHA DANDRIDGE CUSTIS

THIS IS MARTHA AROUND THE TIME SHE MARRIED WASHINGTON.

HOME, SWEET HOME

Washington was happy at Mount Vernon. From 1759 to 1775, he worked 6 days a week to run the estate. He made the house larger. He also experimented with new crops and farming methods.

Washington was active in Virginia government during this time. In 1758, he was elected to the colony's lawmaking body, the House of Burgesses. He served there for 15 years. He became a justice of the peace in 1760, too.

Presidential Preview

A justice of the peace is a judge who can hear less important cases and suggest which other cases should be sent to a higher court. A justice of the peace can also marry people.

This shows an artist's idea of Washington's life at Mount Vernon.

THE WAR FOR INDEPENDENCE

After the French and Indian War ended in 1763, England began taxing its colonies to pay for keeping an army in North America. Angry **colonists** began the American Revolution to fight for their independence in 1775. Washington left Mount Vernon to lead the colonies' military forces.

The war lasted 8 years. At times, it seemed as if Washington's forces would lose to the British. But Washington had become a good leader and finally led the Americans to **victory**. The colonies became the free and independent United States.

Presidential Preview

Before the American Revolution began, Washington was one of Virginia's leaders against British taxes. Like others, he was angry since colonists had no say in the taxes.

This picture was painted of Washington during the American Revolution.

RETURN TO MOUNT VERNON

The American Revolution finally ended in 1783. Washington went to Congress, gave up his military title, and returned to his life at Mount Vernon.

Washington made the house on the estate larger. He created new plans for the grounds. He planted trees and grasses from other countries. He welcomed many guests, including military friends and visitors from other states and countries. Mount Vernon was where Washington was happiest, and he planned to stay there until he died.

Presidential Preview

How does King George Washington sound? Some thought Washington should become king after the war ended, but he refused.

Today, you can visit Mount Vernon and learn about Washington's life there.

HERO, FARMER, PRESIDENT

By 1783, George Washington had come a long way from the boy with a limited education. He had become a hero by leading the colonies to victory in the American Revolution and again for turning down great power. But power didn't interest Washington. He loved farming, and his heart was at Mount Vernon.

However, Washington was soon called away again. In 1787, he oversaw the writing of a new **constitution**. Finally, in 1789, he was elected the first president of the United States.

Presidential Preview

When Washington was elected president in 1789, he thought he had to accept for the good of the country. He wrote that he felt like "a **culprit**, who is going to the place of his **execution**."

Washington's Road to the Presidency

1732 George Washington is born February 22.

1748 He surveys land in the Shenandoah Valley.

1749 He becomes the surveyor of Culpeper County.

1752 His brother Lawrence dies and leaves Mount Vernon to Washington.

1754 The French and Indian War begins. He becomes a military leader for Virginia.

1758 He leaves the Virginia military. He's elected to the Virginia House of Burgesses.

1759 He marries Martha Dandridge Custis.

1760 He becomes a justice of the peace.

1775 He's chosen as leader of the colonial forces during the American Revolution.

1783 He returns to Mount Vernon.

1789 George Washington is elected the first president of the United States.

WASHINGTON'S INAUGURATION

WASHINGTON ON MOUNT RUSHMORE

GLOSSARY

American Revolution: the war from 1775 to 1783 in which the colonies won their freedom from England

civility: polite, reasonable, and respectful behavior

colonist: someone who lives in a colony, which is a piece of land under the control of another country

constitution: the basic laws by which a country or state is governed

culprit: a person who has committed a crime or done something wrong

decent: polite, moral, and honest

estate: a big house in the country on a large piece of land

execution: the act of killing someone especially as punishment for a crime

inherit: to get by legal right after a person's death

surveyor: one whose job is to measure land areas

victory: a win over someone you're fighting against

widow: a woman whose husband has died

FOR MORE INFORMATION

Books

Gilpin, Caroline Crosson. *George Washington.* Washington, DC: National Geographic, 2014.

Gregory, Josh. *George Washington: The 1st President.* New York, NY: Bearport Publishing, 2015.

Websites

Biography: President George Washington
www.ducksters.com/biography/uspresidents/georgewashington.php
Read a short biography of Washington on this website.

George Washington: A National Treasure
www.georgewashington.si.edu
Learn what a famous painting of Washington tells you about the man, and learn about hidden meanings in the painting.

7 Fun Facts About George Washington
www.scholastic.com/teachers/articles/teaching-content/7-fun-facts-about-george-washington/
Find some fun facts about Washington here.

INDEX